A LITTLE SLUGGER'S GUIDE TO THE

UNWRITTEN

Rules of Baseball and Life

BY PATRICK RENNA

PENGUIN WORKSHOP

ILLUSTRATED BY TOMMY PARKER

FOR MY KIDS, FLYNN & LIAM, AND YOURS.
HOPEFULLY THIS BOOK WILL HELP MAKE
BEDTIME NOT GO EXTRA INNINGS—PR

FOR MARIE, WHO ALWAYS KNOCKS IT OUT OF THE PARK—TP

PENGUIN WORKSHOP
An imprint of Penguin Random House LLC
1745 Broadway, New York, New York 10019

First published in the United States of America by Penguin Workshop,
an imprint of Penguin Random House LLC, 2025

Text copyright © 2025 by Patman, Inc.
Illustrations copyright © 2025 by Tommy Parker

Visit us online at penguinrandomhouse.com.

Library of Congress Cataloging-in-Publication Data is available.

Manufactured in China

ISBN 9780593754870   10 9 8 7 6 5 4 3 2 1 HH

Design by Taylor Abatiell

FOR A *SPECIAL* LITTLE SLUGGER:

_____

FROM:

_____

Rule #1: ALWAYS BE READY

In 1993, when I was just thirteen years old, I auditioned for a role in a movie called *The Sandlot*, which ultimately changed the trajectory of my life. Maybe you've seen the movie. If you haven't, go watch it, and then continue reading. I'll wait . . .

Really, I will.

Go make some popcorn and settle into the comfy side of the couch. We're talking, like, ninety minutes here.

Okay, now that you've seen it, you know the movie is set in the summer of 1962, and it's about a new kid in town who makes friends with a group of kids whose sole purpose in life is to play baseball at their local sandlot. But the movie is so much more than just a story about baseball. It's a metaphor for life. It's not about the game or whether you win or lose (hey, that's important, don't get me wrong!). But it's also about the friends you meet and the lessons you learn along the way. It's about the journey.

And one of the many things I've learned on my journey is that being an actor on the set of a movie is, in a way, a lot like being a player on a baseball team, because you learn to play together as a part of an ensemble. Each person—whether it's the pitcher, catcher, director, or camera operator—plays a vital role on the team. And like baseball, where the game changes with each pitch, things on a movie set can change unexpectedly for a variety of reasons. No day on set ever goes as planned, so everyone learns to adapt . . . and quickly!

In the movie, I was cast as Hamilton Porter, the protector of the sandlot whose talent for baseball is matched only by his talent for hurling insults at the opposing team. And that very quotable scene where I hurl those insults, believe it or not, was not written for my character.

It was written for Benny the Jet.

About an hour before we were scheduled to begin shooting the scene, there was a knock on my trailer door. I opened it, and in front of me was the director, David Mickey Evans. I immediately knew something was up, because this was not normal. Even more suspect were the pages of fresh script printed on yellow paper in his hands. Anytime changes are made to a script, the new pages are printed on a different color. But before I could get a word in, David dramatically threw the yellow pages in my direction in a truly director-like fashion and declared, "It's your scene now, so learn your lines!" And just like that he was gone.

At first, I wanted to panic (let's be honest, I did panic). But then I got focused and began learning my new lines and new part . . . fast! Now, look, I may have a natural inclination to talking trash, but he gave me one hour to learn the likes of "You mix your Wheaties with your mama's toe jam!" I learned a very important lesson that day on set—my first unwritten rule to life—which I've carried with me to this very day: Always be ready.

Because no matter how much you plan or prepare, things change. So, it's up to you to always be ready for what the day might bring. And who knows, it just might change the trajectory of your life.

Rule #2: MAGIC IS REAL

Every spring, when the chill of winter begins to give way to warmer weather (unless you live in Los Angeles, where it's seventy-two degrees all year), something magical happens. And you can witness that magic at a baseball game.

If you're lucky enough to go to a professional game, pay attention to your senses: the sights, sounds, smells, feel, and even the tastes of the game. The warm yellow sun hanging in the clear blue sky. The smell of freshly mowed grass in the air. A pennant flag waving in the wind. A vendor calling out, "Ballpark franks! Get your hot dogs here!"

Feel the sticky crunch of Cracker Jack between your teeth and the crack of peanut shells as they open in your fingers. Take off your ball cap, place it over your heart, and listen to one voice singing the national anthem to a silent crowd of fifty thousand people. Listen as the stadium erupts with a roar and applause as the singer holds their final note. Watch the umpire dust home plate and belt out, "Play ball!"

When the batter digs their heels in, waiting for the pitcher to deliver the first pitch, there's another silence. And the only sound is the hum of a split-finger fastball soaring ninety-nine miles per hour through the cool, crisp air.

CRACK!

That's the sound of a baseball meeting a wooden bat, sending the ball over one hundred miles per hour in the opposite direction over the outfield wall and into the stands. Listen as the home crowd erupts again.

And someday, if you practice and work hard, that could be you at the center of the crowd's cheer. And in that moment, you'll know for certain that the magic of baseball is real.

Rule #3: PRACTICE ISN'T OPTIONAL

Now that we've established magic is real and how to experience it, let's talk about something necessary to make that magic happen: practice.

Practice is more than just, well, practice. It's about your commitment to a sport, a goal, or school. Showing up day in and day out prepares you for the big game or the test.

Do your homework and show up to practice and good things will come your way. Not by some stroke of luck, but because you're prepared!

Warming up and stretching your muscles and mind is always a good strategy for success.

Rule #4: DON'T UNDERESTIMATE A GAME OF CATCH* *(OR A WALK OUTSIDE)

Is there anything better than a simple game of catch?

There is something therapeutic about the simplicity of tossing a ball back and forth between two gloves. (BONUS RULE: IT ALSO HELPS WARM UP YOUR ARM.)

So, next time you might be feeling a bit down or stressed out, get outside into the fresh air, and have a nice game of catch with a friend, a sibling, a parent—*whoever!*—and only focus on the ball and your glove. You just might find it may help level you out.

No one to test out the fastball with? Go for a long walk in the great outdoors and imagine you're walking through the corn on the Field of Dreams.

Rule #5: FIND A GLOVE THAT FITS

A big part of being prepared to play is having the right equipment and making sure it fits! You don't want to be that kid wearing a glove two sizes too big.

The same applies to school: Make sure to sharpen your pencils, so to speak, and bring your books. Having the right tools for the job makes the work a lot easier.

Rule #6: KEEP YOUR EYE ON THE BALL

Whether you're up at the plate or have your mind set on another life goal, make sure to keep your eye on the ball.

And if life throws you a curveball, remember, you have three strikes and unlimited foul balls.

(BONUS RULE FOR PARENTS: IF YOU CATCH A FOUL BALL AT A GAME, GIVE IT TO THE KID.)

Rule #7: KEEP SWINGING

When you're first learning the game of baseball—or any sport—keep swinging, literally and figuratively. You're bound to miss, but life's not about the swings and shots you miss, it's about the ones you make.

Consider the story of Harmon Killebrew, nicknamed "Hammerin' Harmon," who played twenty-two seasons in the big leagues. When Killebrew retired, he was second in home runs only to Babe Ruth (yes, *that* Babe Ruth). In 1984, Killebrew was inducted into the Baseball Hall of Fame with a .256 batting average. That means for every ten times he stepped up to the plate, he hit the ball an average of 2.5 times.

So, next time you swing and miss, remember: There's always next at bat.

(BONUS RULE FOR KIDS: IF YOU COME ACROSS A BASEBALL SIGNED BY BABE RUTH, DON'T TOUCH IT.)

Rule #8:
PRACTICE IN SILENCE, PERFORM IN PUBLIC

Question: Is there anything cooler than watching a major leaguer belt a whopping home run and flip their bat in celebration in front of a sold-out stadium?

Answer: Nope, nothing cooler. Kidding! What's cooler is knowing that it took a whole lot of batting practice on empty fields to be able to perform a feat like that in front of a crowd.

So, before you start practicing your bat-flipping skills, make sure to put in good hours at the batting cage.

Rule #9:
BLOCK OUT THE NOISE

And when you're on the metaphorical road to the big game or a big life moment, know that there will be a whole lot of noise along the way. Keep your mind on your goals and your eye on the prize and try to ignore the distractions.

Rule #10: BASEBALL IS A TEAM SPORT

Here's the scene: It's Game One of the 2015 World Series between the Kansas City Royals and the New York Mets. It's 4—4 in the bottom of the fourteenth inning (yep, you read that correctly), and Royals first baseman Eric Hosmer steps up to the plate. It's well past midnight, and the game has been going on for more than five hours.

The Mets pitcher delivers, and Hosmer hits a high fly ball to right field that gets caught for an out. Bummer, right? Wrong!

Hosmer's sacrifice fly allowed his teammate Alcides Escobar to score the game-winning run, giving the Royals the early momentum to ultimately win their franchise's first World Series title in over thirty years.

Sometimes, even when you make an out, you help propel your team to victory. Life is the same way: You have to make sacrifices to ultimately succeed.

Rule #11: "SMALL BALL" IS STILL BALL

Don't underestimate the power of something small like a bunt. Not everything you do in life will be a line-drive double to the wall, if you know what I mean. But a bunt is no easy feat. It requires great skill and focus to execute one flawlessly. And even a bunt can change the outcome of a game and the season.

Rule #12:

FAILURE IS PART OF THE GAME*

*(AND IT'S PART OF LIFE!)

Michael Jordan might be best known as the GOAT of basketball. But Jordan once famously retired from basketball to try his hand at the game of baseball, where he played one season with the Birmingham Barons, the Double-A minor league affiliate for the Chicago White Sox.

And here's what Jordan has said about failure: "I've missed more than nine thousand shots in my career. I've lost almost three hundred games. Twenty-six times I've been trusted to take the game-winning shot and missed. I've failed over and over and over again in my life. And that is why I succeed."

A hitter's biggest challenge is staying confident after a strikeout . . . or even worse, a hitting slump. When you accept that failing is part of baseball and part of life, you'll learn from your mistakes and quickly adjust to break out of that slump.

Don't think of losing as a failure. Losing is an opportunity to do better and improve.

Rule #13:
TREAT YOUR TEAMMATES WITH RESPECT*

*(AND LIFT THEM UP WHEN THEY ARE FEELING DOWN)

You know what's worse than giving up a home run or dropping an easy pop-up that scores a run? Having your teammates rag on you for making that error. Mistakes are part of the game.

A great player supports their teammates through thick and thin. And a great team learns to come together after giving up a homer or an error and still win the game.

The same goes for family, friends, neighbors, and teachers. Treat others with respect and be there for them when they need help. And next time you need help, they'll do the same for you.

Rule #14:
BE NICE TO THE NEW KID*

Someday you'll be one, too. Kindness and karma are boomerangs, so make sure to share some and it'll come back around to you when you need it most.

*(EVEN BABE RUTH WAS THE NEW KID ONCE!)

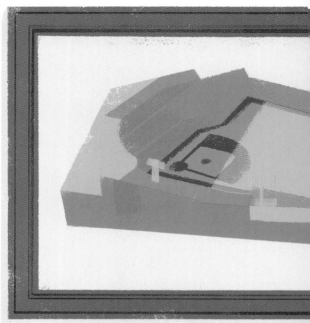

Rule #15: BE DIFFERENT

Like life, the game of baseball is all about embracing, accepting, and celebrating differences. Just think about all the various stadiums. The ivy that climbs up the walls of Wrigley Field. The harbor that edges up against Oracle Park. The Green Monster in Fenway that swallows up would-be homers for right-handed hitters. The short porch at Yankee Stadium that favors lefty hitters. The list goes on. The point is each stadium is as unique as the very fans that sit in its seats and the players on the field. And the game is still played the exact same way.

The best players learn to adapt to each stadium's differences and even use them to their advantage. And sometimes, life deals you a pitch you don't want to swing at. But if you learn to see and approach life a bit differently, good things can come your way.

Rule #16: BE THE UNDERDOG

Don't let other people tell you what is possible. Only you can set your limits . . . and break them.

Consider the story of former Major League Baseball (MLB) pitcher Jim Abbott, who was born without a right hand. In 1991, Abbott placed third in the voting for the American League Cy Young, the most prestigious award for pitchers. In 1993, Abbott threw a no-hitter! And in 1999, Abbott recorded two hits in just twenty-one plate appearances.

When he was growing up, Abbott's disability inspired him to work even harder than most players would: "As a kid I really wanted to fit in. Sports became a way for me to gain acceptance. I think this fueled my desire to succeed. I truly believe that difficult times and disappointments can push us to find abilities and strengths we wouldn't know existed without the experience of struggle."

Believe in yourself, and others will, too.

Rule #17: IT'S A MARATHON, NOT A SPRINT

The beauty of a baseball game is there is no time limit. Sure, there is a pitching clock now, but barring a weather delay, the game ends after at least nine innings are played. And unlike football and basketball, whose regular seasons have 17 and 82 games respectively, baseball is a grueling 162-game regular season that typically spans from April until October. So, when in doubt, zoom out and look at the bigger picture. Even if your team lost one game or you had one bad day, there's always tomorrow and the day after that and the day after that and the . . . you get the picture.

Rule #18: GIVE IT YOUR ALL

As long as you give it your all, you can never be disappointed—even if you lose. Play every game like it's bottom of the ninth, two outs, and the game is on the line. Sometimes you might come up short and sometimes things are simply out of your control. But what you can control is the effort and dedication you put into something. And that is a victory in itself, and you should feel good about that. After the game, whether you win or lose, get a good night's sleep, because tomorrow is a new day.

Rule #19: IT'S ABOUT THE JOURNEY

Sure, we all want to win the game. After all, that's why we suit up and play, right? But there's more to baseball or any sport than just a victory. It's about all the moments—the people you meet, the friends you make, the times you fail, the lessons you learn—that add up to something much more valuable than any victory. The real enjoyment and experience of baseball—and life—are those little moments that amount to something so great you can't even begin to put it into words.

So, lace up your cleats, put on a glove that fits, and find yourself a field, a diamond, a sandlot, even an empty parking lot will do, and go play a game of baseball with friends. You just might find some magic out there.

Rule #20:
DON'T BE AFRAID TO CALL
(AND TAKE) YOUR SHOT

Baseball, like life, is about seeing an opportunity and taking it. So, make sure to always be ready, and when opportunity knocks, open up the door. It could change the rest of your life.